ROOMS OUTSIDE THE HOUSE

FROM GAZEBOS TO GARDEN ROOMS

ROOMS OUTSIDE THE HOUSE

FROM GAZEBOS TO GARDEN ROOMS

James Grayson Trulove

HD
HARPER
DESIGN

An Imprint of HarperCollins*Publishers*

ROOMS OUTSIDE THE HOUSE

Copyright 2005 © by James Grayson Trulove and Harper Design

First published in 2005 by
Harper Design
An Imprint of HarperCollins*Publishers*
10 East 53rd Street
New York, NY 10022
Tel: (212) 207-7000
Fax: (212) 207-7654
HarperDesign@harpercollins.com
www.harpercollins.com

Distributed throughout the world by:
HarperCollins International
10 East 53rd Street
New York, NY 10022
Fax: (212) 207-7654

HarperCollins books may be purchased for educational, business, or sales promotional use.
For information, please write: Special Markets Department, HarperCollins Publishers Inc.,
10 East 53rd Street, New York, NY 10022.

Packaged by:
Grayson Publishing, LLC
James G. Trulove, Publisher
1250 28th Street NW
Washington, DC 20007
202-337-1380
jtrulove@aol.com
Graphic Design by: Agnieszka Stachowicz

Library of Congress Control Number: 2005922572

ISBN: 0-06-074981-4

Manufactured in China
First printing, 2005
1 2 3 4 5 6 7 8 9 / 08 07 06 05

CONTENTS

FOREWORD

FOR THOSE FORTUNATE ENOUGH TO HAVE SOME LAND EXTENDING BEYOND THE FOOTPRINT OF THEIR HOUSE, the possibilities of life outside the box are limited only by the imagination. Whatever the climate or the budget, adventure awaits in the back yard in the form of gazebos, workshops, dining pavilions, saunas, pool houses, guest houses—even honey houses. Go below ground and build a wine cellar, or out on the ranch for a party barn, or up into the sky for a studio above the garage. Live in a part of the country where insects rule? A bug house may be the solution to enjoying the outdoors. An outdoor dining pavilion is a must when summering on the Maine coast or by your own swimming pool. ▪ The serious minded will find an essential home office located a few steps from the house essential for a productive day. When evening comes, it can magically be transformed into a hangout for family and friends. And when temperatures in the far northern reaches of the country drop into the minus category, a dash through the snow to a hot, welcoming sauna is invigorating. If you are feeling cramped in your present house, there is no need to move. Simply build a party barn and dance the night away. ▪ As for a honey house . . . read on!

LEFT: A barn converted into a music studio (Centerbrook Architects; Woodruff/Brown, photographer)
RIGHT: A dining pavilion beside the vegetable garden (El Dorado; Michael Sinclair, photographer)

LEFT: Jars of honey on display in the Honey House (Marlon Blackwell Architect; Richard Leo Johnson, photographer) RIGHT: A wine cellar for storage and entertaining (Miro Rivera Architects; Christopher Lovi, photographer) BELOW RIGHT: Every house needs a party barn (Shipley Architects; Charles Davis Smith, photographer).

PROJECTS

BARNES **POOL** HOUSE

THIS 1050-SQUARE-FOOT POOL HOUSE SERVES AT TIMES AS A WEEKEND residence. It is located near the crest of a hill about 800 feet above the Napa Valley floor. Incorporating the view into the design was a major consideration. The pool house has a simple shed roof that expands out and up, opening the space inside to the sky. The glass wall folds away, allowing the slate deck plane to run into the building. The shower has a sliding glass door that allows for showering outside as well. The water level of the pool is held only an inch below the deck, running out to an infinite edge on both sides. ▪ Building materials were chosen to create a color palette complimentary to the natural landscape. The Pau Lope wood fencing that hides the cars will weather to a soft neutral gray. The slate is a mottled composition of iron oxides layered over greens and grays, blending nicely with the color of the Napa Valley clay soil. The stucco walls are a warm mustard color and the Corten steel roof and copper trim have oxidized out into mottled tones of brown. Only the pool is dark, which emphasizes the mirror effect of the water's surface.

ARCHITECT ▪ **LUNDBERG DESIGN**
PHOTOGRAPHER ▪ **CESAR RUBIO**
LOCATION ▪ **SAN FRANCISCO, CALIFORNIA**

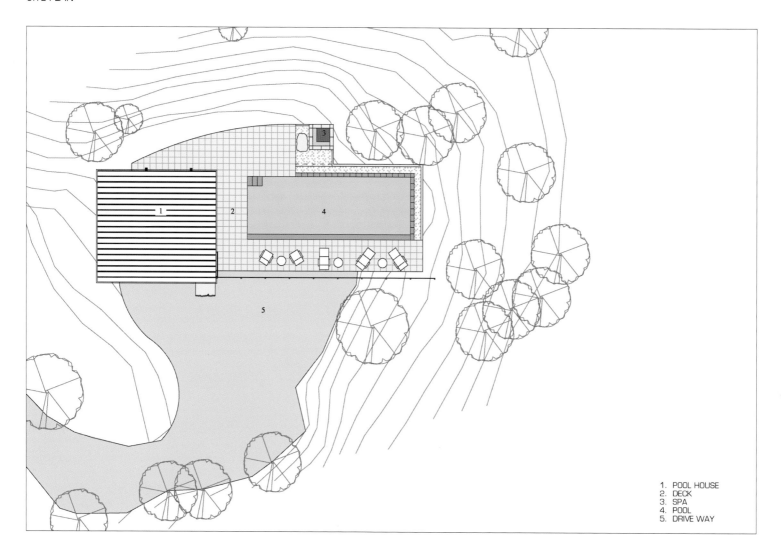

1. POOL HOUSE
2. DECK
3. SPA
4. POOL
5. DRIVE WAY

PREVIOUS PAGES: The dark surface of the pool reflects the light from the pool house and from the sky. RIGHT: Sliding doors provide the option of showering inside or outside. FAR RIGHT: The entry to the pool from the parking area is screened by wooden fencing.

ABOVE AND RIGHT: The goal of the design was to bring the outdoors inside.

LEFT AND ABOVE: The shed roof flips up to open the interior to the sky.

GUEST HOUSE & PARTY BARN

A freestanding, two-story bedroom tower and a single-story party barn with kitchen and bunkroom complete a modest compound of farm structures two hours southwest of Dallas. The party barn is designed to be pavilion-like. On two sides there are overhead garage doors that roll up to the exterior to nest under the porch roofs. The upper walls of the exterior of this building are covered in corrugated gavalume metal. The lower walls are clad in clear, corrugated PVC panels that are layered with perforated, corrugated metal that brings diffused light into the interior. The upper walls are clad with oil-finished pine flooring boards. The stone mantle and the hearthstone were cut from slabs from a nearby creek. ▪ Each guest bedroom is 12-by-18 feet and painted white with simple linen shades on the windows. The bedroom windows look out onto a peach orchard. A small addition was built to house a mud porch, a laundry room, a bathroom, and a screened porch.

ARCHITECT ▪ **SHIPLEY ARCHITECTS**
PHOTOGRAPHER ▪ **CHARLES DAVIS SMITH**
LOCATION ▪ **HICO, TEXAS**

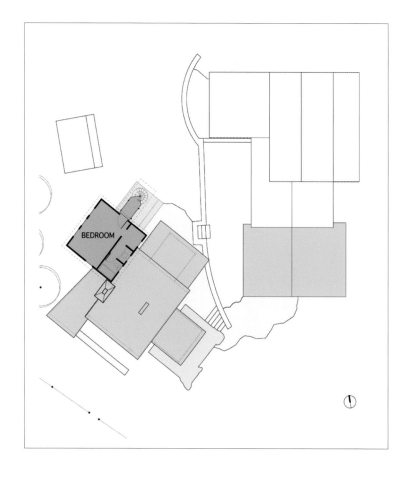

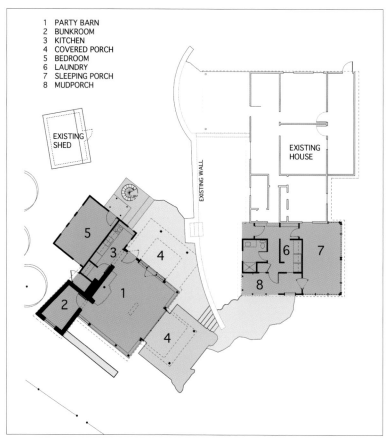

1 PARTY BARN
2 BUNKROOM
3 KITCHEN
4 COVERED PORCH
5 BEDROOM
6 LAUNDRY
7 SLEEPING PORCH
8 MUDPORCH

EXISTING SHED

EXISTING WALL

EXISTING HOUSE

BEDROOM

PREVIOUS PAGES: The lower half of the party barn is clad in clear, corrugated PVC panels that are layered with perforated, corrugated metal, giving the building a glow at night. LEFT: Every effort was made to carefully integrate the new addition with the existing farm house. RIGHT: A 400-square-foot utility space was added to the existing house. ABOVE RIGHT: View of the party barn and guest tower beyond

ABOVE AND RIGHT: Oil-finished pine floor boards add warmth to the interior of the party barn. FOLLOWING PAGES: The design and materials of the guest house and party barn are influenced by the vernacular architecture.

BROADFORD FARMS PAVILION

THIS PAVILION AND POOL ARE PART OF A LARGER COMPLEX SURROUNDED by 120 acres of aspen and cottonwood forest that bends along two miles of the Big Wood River in Idaho. The structure's orientation offers dramatic views of bordering mountains to the west and to the distant south, while maintaining its visual connection to the main compound 200 yards away. During the summer months, the prevailing breezes cool and ventilate the pavilion, which consists of a lounging area, a changing room, and a bath and shower area. The total area, including decks and the mechanical enclosure, is just under 1800 square feet. The pavilion itself is 645 square feet. ▪ Building materials consist of recycled Douglas fir, galvanized corrugated steel roofing, and Ipé wood siding and decking.

ARCHITECT ▪ LAKE/FLATO ARCHITECTS
PHOTOGRAPHER ▪ BRIAN KORTE
LOCATION ▪ HAILEY, IDAHO

LEGEND

1 LIVING AREA
2 SHOWER
3 BATH / CHANGING
4 MECHANICAL
5 POOL EQUIP

0 5 10 20

PREVIOUS PAGES AND RIGHT: The pavilion and pool rest in a clearing of native grasses and trees that funnel the views toward the nearby hillside. BELOW: A Kalwall panel above the shower brings light into the oiled Ipé enclosure.

LEFT: In the summer, the pavilion merges with nature.

ABOVE AND RIGHT: The pavilion has wood siding and decking with galvanized corrugated steel roofing.

LEFT: A walkway connects the pavilion to the mechanical room.

EMERSON SAUNA

ON FINNISH IMMIGRANTS' PIONEER FARMSTEADS IN THE UNITED STATES, the sauna was often the first building erected and became the social center. The the clients for this project, who were reared in northern Minnesota's Scandinavian culture, wanted to revive this social aspect of the sauna. The interior of the sauna has brick walls with Douglas fir ceilings, doors, benches, and cabinets. It has a flat, sod-covered roof to hold the heat. Cantelivered above and extending outward is a Douglas fir-paneled cooling room with a steeply pitched roof. It is open at both ends to allow breezes to flow through, yet its second-floor location provides privacy. It is supported by a curved brick wall that encloses a shower.

ARCHITECT ▪ **SALMELA ARCHITECTS**
PHOTOGRAPHER ▪ **PETER KERZE**
LOCATION ▪ **DULUTH, MINNESOTA**

ELEVATIONS

FLOOR PLANS

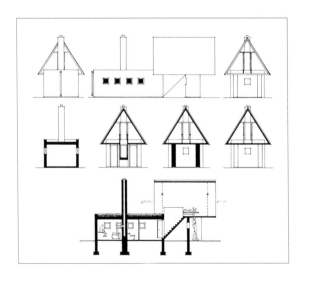

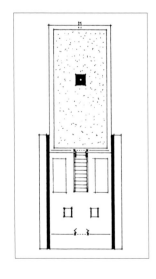

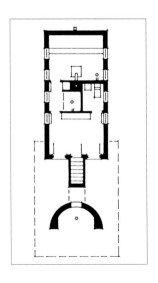

SOD ROOF DETAIL

COOLING ROOM ROOF DETAIL

PREVIOUS PAGES: The long, narrow sauna has a sod roof. Logs for the sauna's heater are stored along the side. ABOVE: The second-floor cooling room is supported by a curved brick wall that encloses a sauna.

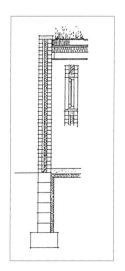

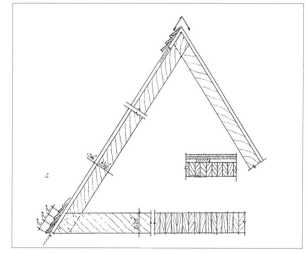

LEFT: A view across the roof of the sauna and through the cooling room
BELOW: A slender brick chimney extends above the sauna and punctuates
the elegant, simple profile of the sauna.

ABOVE AND ABOVE RIGHT: The interior of the sauna has brick walls, Douglas fir ceilings and
benches, and slate floors. FAR RIGHT: The stairway to the second floor cooling room
FOLLOWING PAGES: Interior and exterior views of the Douglas fir-paneled cooling room

MAINE DINING PAVILION

ON AN ISLAND OFF THE COAST OF MAINE, THIS DINING PAVILION IS LOCATED on the edge of a meadow looking out across Penobscot Bay. The back wall is made of native stone and is pressed into the hillside. Inside the pavilion, the wall forms the chimney, fireplace, and two storage cabinets. The clerestory panels and doors are made of local white cedar and are fastened with gudgeon and pintle hardware, which is typically used in fence construction. The doors are opened and closed using cane bolts, another garden fence element. The louvered French doors provide a sense of enclosure while allowing light and the sea air to permeate. A canvas and steel canopy structure gives shelter and shade while recalling a boat's hull in form. Rainwater drains from its edge into a gravel ring in the floor. Hand-carved text in the stone floor speaks of the building's relationship to its environment, with the four directions marked "EARTH, AIR, FIRE, and WATER." A tree is planted in each corner to bring the outdoors closer. Dinners and gatherings take place around an eight-foot granite table with all the necessary accessories and supplies stowed neatly in the storage cupboards behind.

ARCHITECT ▪ SAMUEL H. WILLIAMSON ASSOCIATES
PHOTOGRAPHER ▪ BRIAN VANDEN BRINK
LOCATION ▪ NORTH HAVEN, MAINE

SITE PLAN

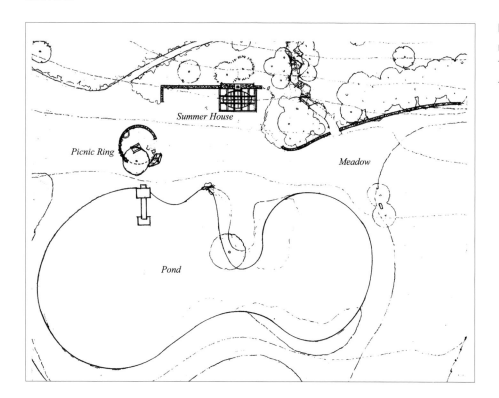

Summer House

Picnic Ring

Meadow

Pond

PREVIOUS PAGES: Rainwater from the canvas roof drains into the gravel ring on the floor, encircling the dining table. BELOW AND BELOW LEFT: The storage cupboards in the open and closed positions RIGHT: Dining takes place around an eight-foot slab of granite.

ABOVE AND LEFT: The white cedar louvered doors provide a sense of enclosure. FOLLOWING PAGES: The dining pavilion is tucked into the hillside and enjoys views over a pond and the bay beyond.

POOLSIDE GAZEBO

BUILT ADJACENT TO A FARM HOUSE, THIS POOL HOUSE WAS DESIGNED to enclose an existing structure, as well as provide a covered seating area and a small kitchen. ■ The dual orientation of the pool house provides a focal point for the living room, which has a long curved wall of windows, and acts as a terminus for the drive up to the house. The covered seating is in a gazebo that faces the house. The pool house roof rises up gradually to cover it. Three feet from the existing building's face a new façade, consisting of a lattice screen that extends across the pool house's old windows and door, allows them to remain unchanged. At the façade's center, an entrance and chimney connect the pool house to the axis of the drive, providing a satisfying new focus to the drive's extraordinary alley of trees.

ARCHITECT ■ **CHAD FLOYD, CENTERBROOK ARCHITECTS**
               & PLANNERS
PHOTOGRAPHER ■ **NORMAN McGRATH**
LOCATION ■ **CONNECTICUT**

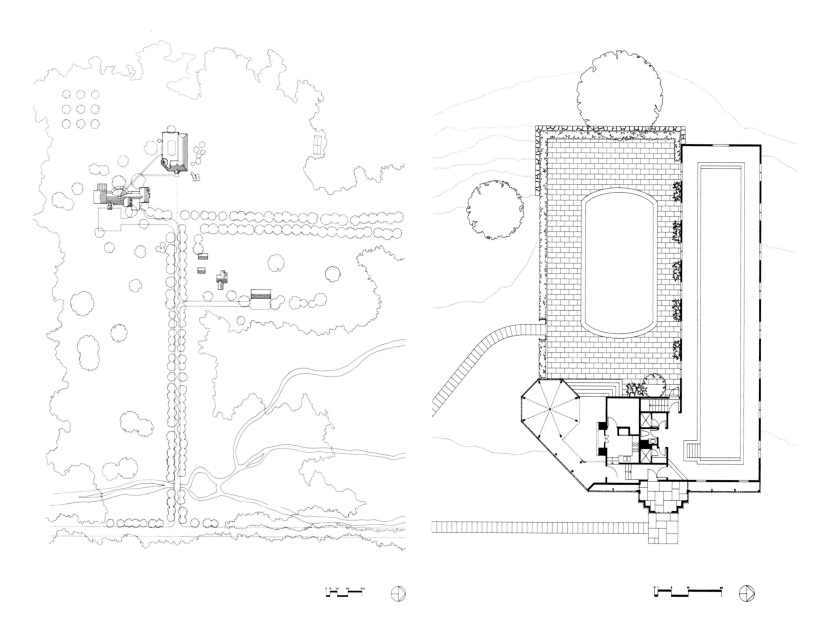

PREVIOUS PAGES: The roof covering the pool house gradually rises to enclose the gazebo. RIGHT: A view of the gazebo FOLLOWING PAGES: A view of the main entrance to the pool house

STUDIO, GARAGE, AND GUEST HOUSE

REPLACING A ONE-STORY GARAGE WITH A NEW STRUCTURE TO INCLUDE A garage, guest quarters, and an artist's studio was complicated even further by the desire to preserve a large tree whose roots were intertwined with the site. The solution was to preserve the old garage foundation and pierce it with new piers to support the second-floor construction. The ground floor area, restricted by the tree trunk, alley, pool, and driveway, is smaller than the second floor, forcing the second floor to overhang in one direction while the tree canopy displaces it in another. The studio roof cantilevers to cover the exterior stairs.

ARCHITECT ▪ **SHIPLEY ARCHITECTS**
PHOTOGRAPHERS ▪ **JAMES F. WILSON, DEBORA HUNTER**
LOCATION ▪ **DALLAS, TEXAS**

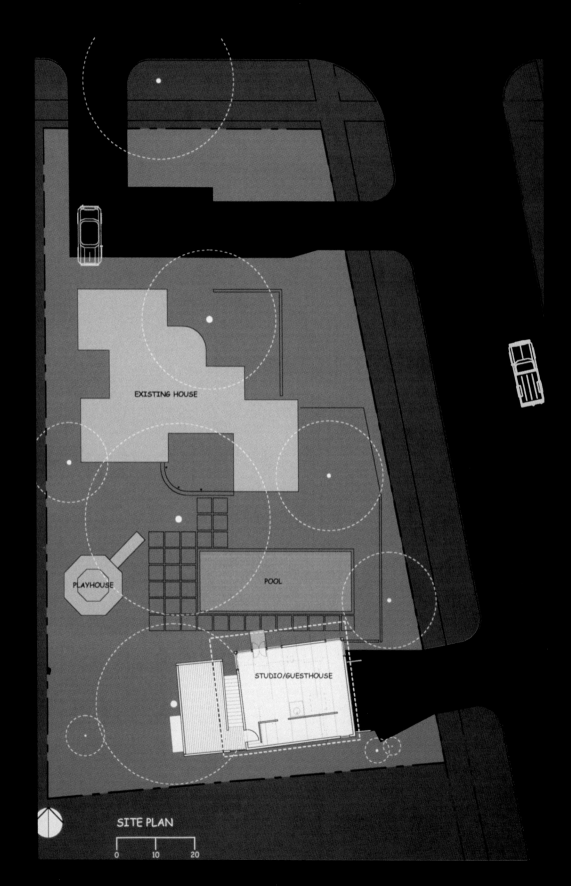

EXISTING HOUSE

PLAYHOUSE

POOL

STUDIO/GUESTHOUSE

SITE PLAN

0   10   20

2nd FLOOR PLAN

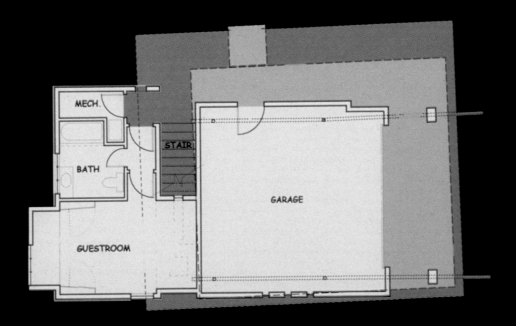

1st FLOOR PLAN

PREVIOUS PAGES AND BELOW: The studio and guest house cantilever over the garage; the exterior is clad in job-formed metal shingles. RIGHT: The exterior stairway to the studio

ABOVE: Extensive glazing was used on the pool side; the corrugated
playhouse to the right was also designed by the architects. ABOVE RIGHT:
A view into the guest quarters

ABOVE: The roof of the studio is constructed of structural insulated panels resting on Microllam rafters. LEFT: Entry to the guest house

BUG SHELTER

SCREENED ON ALL SIDES, INCLUDING THE ROOF, THIS PAVILION WAS designed to be a backyard destination in lieu of a swimming pool, which is a more typical backyard feature in this scorchingly hot climate. But bugs are also a menace here and this shelter provides the necessary protection while the occupants read, nap, or enjoy a snack. It is also a place from which the owners can admire their new home, also designed by Shipley Architects. ▪ Rather than make the roof of the shelter solid and more weather proof, it was decided that only bugs would be excluded—rain, wind, and sunlight are free to enter. ▪ The screened roof is sloped, making it easier to clean the roof with a leaf-blower. The rectangles of copper insect screen are delineated by mahogany framing that supports the screen material. Steel angles form the perimeter of the pavilion.

ARCHITECT ▪ **SHIPLEY ARCHITECTS**
PHOTOGRAPHER ▪ **CHARLES DAVIS SMITH**
LOCATION ▪ **DALLAS, TEXAS**

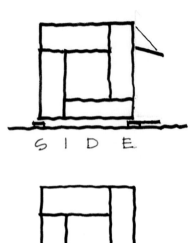

S I D E

F R O N T

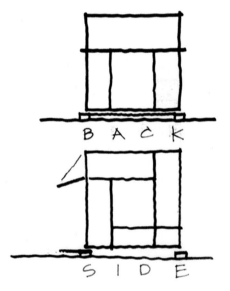

B A C K

S I D E

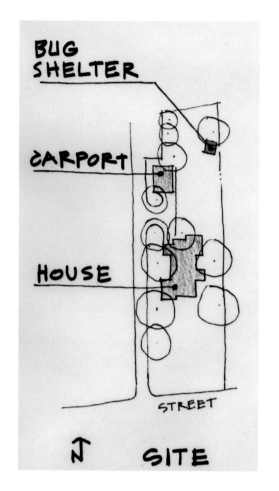

BUG
SHELTER

CARPORT

HOUSE

STREET

N SITE

PREVIOUS PAGES: The slope of the roof is not apparent from the house.
BELOW: The finished product is remarkably like an earlier concept sketch.

LEFT: A detail of the steel and mahogany framing RIGHT: The house can be seen from the pavilion, which is placed at the rear of the backyard.

ABOVE AND RIGHT: The pavilion was conceived as a cube with a sloping screened roof. FOLLOWING PAGES: The pavilion floats above the lawn on concrete footers.

LOKEN BARN & SAUNA

THE LOKEN BARN AND SAUNA ARE TWO OF A COMPLEX OF BUILDINGS overlooking Lake Superior north of Duluth, Minnesota. The barn is a functioning stable for horses as well as for hay storage for the winter feeding season. The barn also serves as a gate house for the compound. The most striking feature of the building is the roof form that wraps and contains the building. The roof consists of finely installed lap board cedar and is steeply pitched to reduce heavy snow loads in this extreme northern climate. ▪ The wet sauna is a combination of a steam room and a hot tub room. The steam room is small with two windows for fresh air and cross ventilation to dry out the room after its use. The tub room and changing area is much larger and taller, with several windows providing views of the tall adjacent spruce trees. There are cooling areas with built-in benches on the two exterior sides of the sauna. The all-cedar structure also has a cedar lap board roof that is exposed on the interior.

ARCHITECT ▪ **SALMELA ARCHITECTS**
PHOTOGRAPHER ▪ **PETER KERZE**
LOCATION ▪ **DULUTH, MINNESOTA**

PREVIOUS PAGES AND RIGHT:
The dramatic cedar lap board roof
wraps and protects the barn.

ELEVATIONS

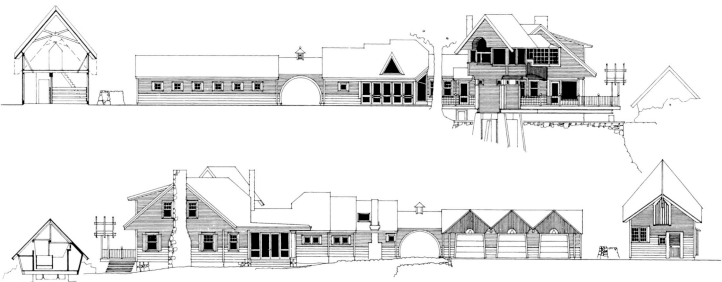

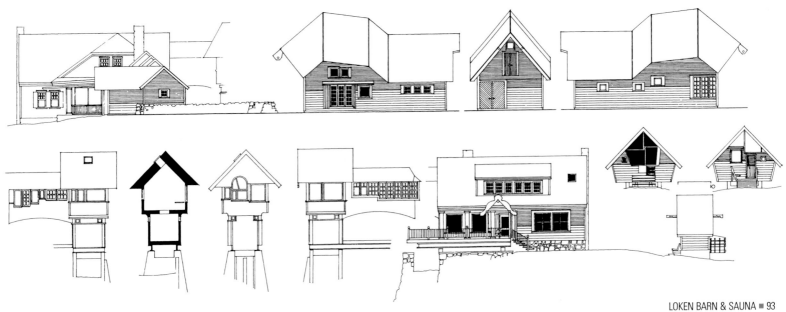

ABOVE AND RIGHT: Ample windows create a bright and welcoming environment for the animals inside.

RIGHT: The all-cedar sauna has cooling areas on either end of the building.

LEFT: The sauna is a welcoming sight during the cold winters.

LEFT AND ABOVE: The large changing room and hot tub area has windows
that invite the exterior woodland inside.

GILBERT/BARKER POD

THE DESIGN AND CONSTRUCTION FOR THIS 288-SQUARE-FOOT DETACHED home office reflect the client's desire for low impact living. Early designs included a planted roof that was later replaced with a PVC membrane and gravel ballast due to cost concerns. The siding is a corrugated copper rain screen. Inside, two partially subterranean rooms are cooled by cross ventilation and heated by a radiant concrete slab fed from the main house. Thick, twelve-inch walls and roof cavities are super-insulated as is the concrete formwork. Photovoltaic panels mounted on the main house provide supplemental power. ■ Translucent polycarbonate cladding on the end wall provides ample natural light during the day and indirect, temperature-adjusted fluorescent lighting provides supplemental lighting. The translucent wall provides diffuse light to illuminate the pathway to the main house at night.

ARCHITECT ■ **EL DORADO, INC.**
PHOTOGRAPHER ■ **JAMIE DARNELL**
LOCATION ■ **JERICHO, VERMONT**

LEFT: The entry leads down to the partially submerged office. RIGHT: Window frames are painted red to frame the landscape. The translucent wall floods the interior with light during the day.

POOL HOUSE AND DECK

THIS NEW 1400-SQUARE-FOOT POOL HOUSE WAS AN ADDITION TO AN existing wood-frame house with a swimming pool. The architects designed a new deck to go around the pool and unite the backyard of the house. The pool house became the east edge of the courtyard, which curls up and around to define the pool house. The cedar deck wraps up to form the pool house. Within the pool house is an intensely-colored blue plaster wall, symbolically pulling the pool into the interior. It runs the length of the addition and is visible from outside. A copper wall connects the hall to the façade of the existing house, which was stained to match the pool house.

ARCHITECT ▪ HANRAHAN AND MEYERS

PHOTOGRAPHER ▪ PETER ARRON, ESTO

LOCATION ▪ LONG ISLAND, NEW YORK

COMPUTER MODEL

FLOOR PLAN/SITE PLAN

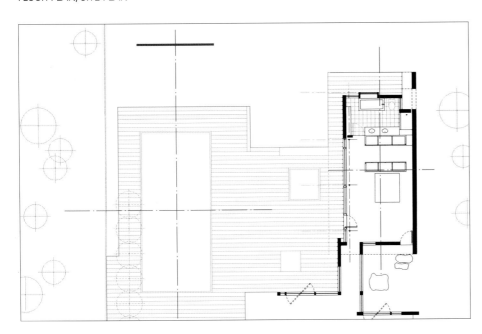

PREVIOUS PAGES: A new cedar deck links the new pool house with the existing house beyond. RIGHT: A hallway connects the pool house to the main house. FOLLOWING PAGES: Inside the pool house, a vigorous blue plaster wall runs the length of the structure.

HOME OFFICE

THIS HOME OFFICE IS A SIMPLE, DETACHED BUILDING NESTLED IN THE OAKS 200 feet from the main house. The siting respects the surrounding landscape, capturing views of Mt. Hood and the valley beyond. During the day, it provides a private place to work and at the end of the day, becomes a casual gathering place for family and friends. The structure has a concrete floor, plywood interior, laminate beams, maple trim, wood windows, and standard "off the shelf" doors. The color of the exterior cementitious board was chosen to blend in with the rich red color of the soil and surrounding vegetation. ■ For the design, there were no drawings and only one site visit. All design issues were resolved using sketches and telephone conferences.

ARCHITECT ■ **PRENTISS ARCHITECTS**
PHOTOGRAPHER ■ **GEOFFREY T. PRENTISS**
LOCATION ■ **SEATTLE, WASHINGTON**

PREVIOUS PAGES: The home office is a center for work and socializing. ABOVE AND RIGHT: The burnt red cementious board was chosen to blend with the soil. The windows and doors are lightly stained.

LEFT: Detail of exterior windows RIGHT: The interior belies the small size of the building. Ample windows provide "borrowed views" of Mt. Hood in the distance. BELOW RIGHT: Detail of the laminate beams and lighting

TAYLOR PAVILION

THE KANSAS CITY, MISSOURI AREA IS KNOWN LOCALLY FOR ITS ROLLING landscape, its fertile soil, and its voracious seasonal insect population. The clients for this 250-square-foot dining pavilion, located on a 120-acre farm north of Kansas City, are avid gardeners. After a few seasons of enjoying their vegetable garden in the open air about a quarter of a mile from their house, the clients decided to take the necessary action to be able to enjoy their hard work without the disruption of summer insects, both flying and crawling. The dining pavilion was constructed adjacent to the garden to provide the perfect solution. Using common building materials, the architects designed, fabricated, and acted as general contractor for this small project.

ARCHITECT ▪ EL DORADO, INC.
PHOTOGRAPHER ▪ MICHAEL SINCLAIR
LOCATION ▪ KANSAS CITY, MISSOURI

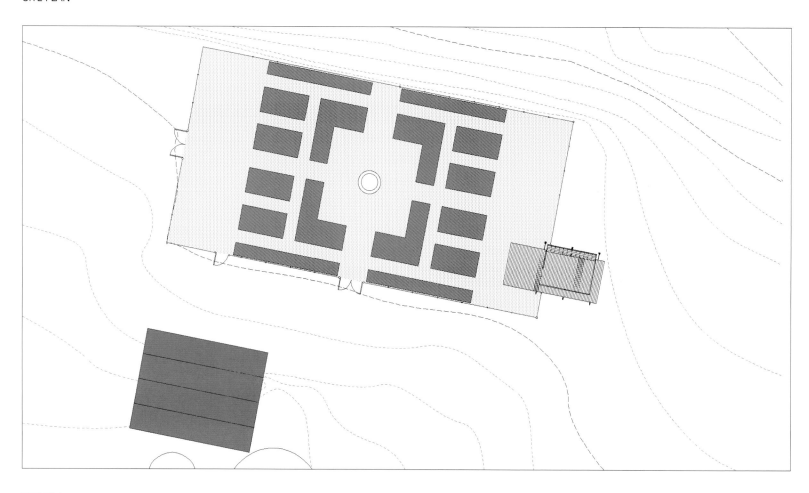

PREVIOUS PAGES: Resting on concrete piers, the pavilion has aluminum mesh walls and ironwood decking. LEFT AND RIGHT: Appropriately, the dining pavilion is located adjacent to the vegetable garden. FOLLOWING PAGES: From the inside, diners enjoy sweeping views of the the rural landscape and the bountiful garden.

TEXAS POOL HOUSE

LOCATED BEHIND A HOUSE OVERLOOKING A TREE-FILLED CANYON, THE shape and location of this pool house and terrace provide a unified and contained outdoor space. From the back porch of the house, a curved stair connects to the terrace below. A fountain and spa cascade down from the porch, providing a visual connection between the main house and the pool. ▪ The terrace offers ample space for outdoor entertaining while maintaining an intimate scale. From here, one enters the upper floor of the pool house, which integrates functions such as the pool, the bath, and the outdoor bar concealed behind sliding doors. The main interior spaces of the pool house open to one another and the canyon view beyond. The curving trellis, which rests on the cantilevered beams radiating from the living room ceiling, becomes a unifying element that provides shade to both interior and exterior living spaces. It wraps over the freestanding barbecue island to provide a shady space for grilling and poolside entertaining.

ARCHITECT ▪ MIRÒ RIVERA ARCHITECTS
PHOTOGRAPHER ▪ PAUL BARDAGJY
LOCATION ▪ AUSTIN, TEXAS

CONCEPT SKETCHES

WEST ELEVATION

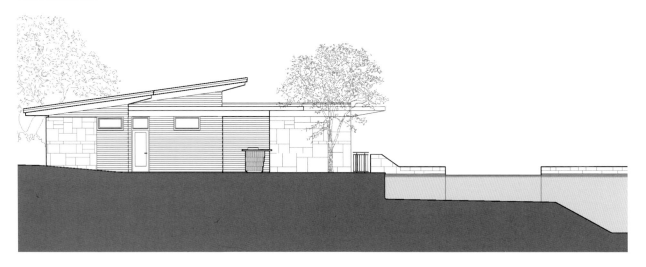

UPPER-LEVEL FLOOR PLAN

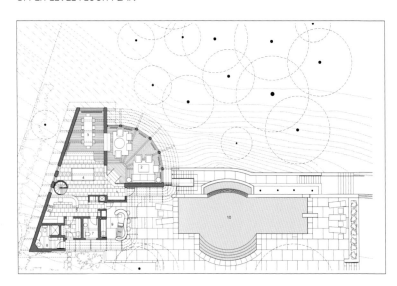

LOWER-LEVEL FLOOR PLAN

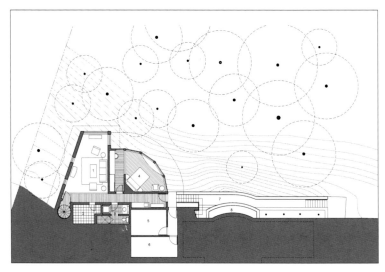

PREVIOUS PAGES: The trellis meanders around the pool house to provide shade for interior and exterior spaces, including the free-standing barbecue island. ABOVE: The sun generates a shifting pattern of light and shadow that animates the pool house's stone walls and terrace throughout the day.

ABOVE: The pool-side bar RIGHT: The exterior siding is Douglas fir;
the pool decking and walls are made of limestone.

ABOVE: Heavy Douglas fir beams and decking are left exposed at the ceiling. RIGHT: The kitchen on the upper level FAR RIGHT: A detail of the spiral stair to the lower-level guest quarters FOLLOWING PAGES: The living room view is oriented toward the rolling green hills of the canyon rather than the pool; a view of the pool and pool house at dusk.

MUSIC STUDIO

THE CLIENT, A PROFESSIONAL VIOLINIST, ENGAGED THE ARCHITECTS TO renovate a barn on her property into a music studio. Several years earlier, the same architects had expanded and renovated her house. She wanted the studio, like the house, to be full of natural light and open to the landscape. The client's Japanese heritage and love of the violin were influential factors in the final design, which blends the character of Japanese farm buildings and country buildings of southern Connecticut. Inside, wooden ceiling panels echo the curve of a violin and provide excellent acoustics. The entrance canopy continues this motif. ▪ As part of the conversion, the barn's eaves were extended and windows were added but the roof and walls were left intact to meet the modest budget.

ARCHITECT ▪ JAMES C. CHILDRESS, CENTERBROOK
ARCHITECTS & PLANNERS
PHOTOGRAPHER ▪ WOODRUFF/BROWN PHOTOGRAPHY
LOCATION ▪ CONNECTICUT

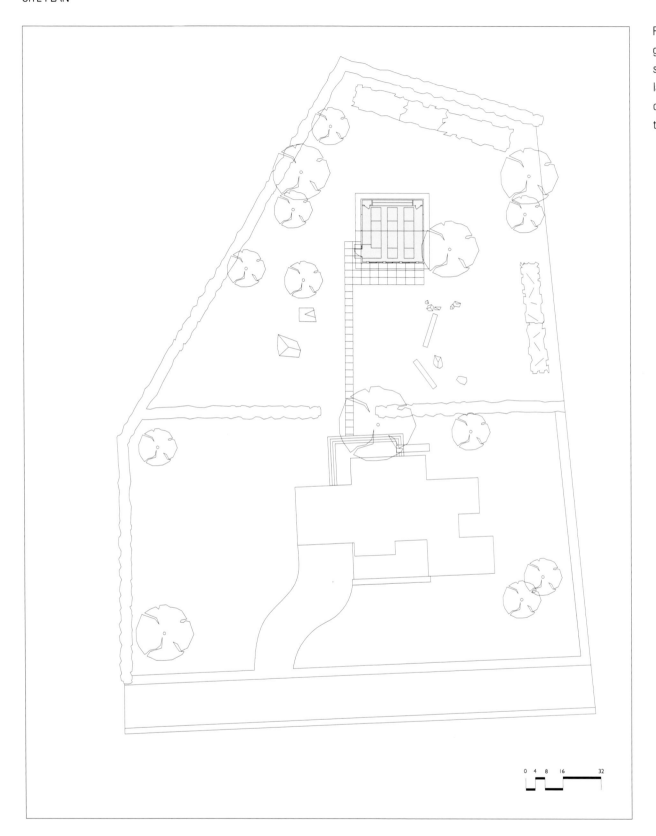

PREVIOUS PAGES: Extensive glazing connects the music studio to the bucolic Connecticut landscape. RIGHT: The awning over the door echoes the curve of the violin.

0 4 8   16   32

LEFT AND RIGHT: The wooden panels that line the ceiling improve the acoustics in the studio. FOLLOWING PAGES: The round windows at either end of the studio draw the eye to the surrounding landscape while conforming to the curvature of the violin body.

WAINWRIGHT WOOD STUDIO

THE CONSTRUCTION OF THIS 1200-SQUARE-FOOT STUDIO FOR A WOOD sculptor is simple and straightforward, consisting of a skeleton of built-up wood frames within a skin of galvanized metal. The frames are made of microlaminated wood with a 2-foot by 6-foot tongue-and-groove roof deck covered in 16-gauge corrugated, galvanized steel—the same material used in highway culverts. An oversized monitor with polycarbonate glazing brings soft, diffused northern light into the studio. The east-facing wall is sheathed in the same material, bringing in additional light. A large window and attached porch visually and physically extend the interior space into the wooded site. A crane rail overhead allows the owner to joist heavy logs used for sculpting.

ARCHITECT ▪ **FRANK HARMON ARCHITECTS**
PHOTOGRAPHER ▪ **JAMES WEST**
LOCATION ▪ **DURHAM, NORTH CAROLINA**

AXONOMETRIC PERSPECTIVE

AXONOMETRIC PERSPECTIVE

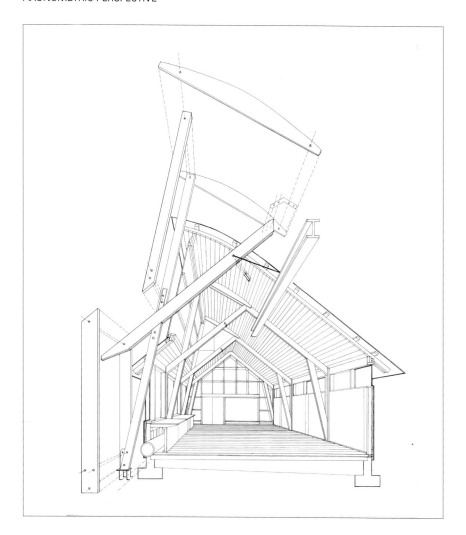

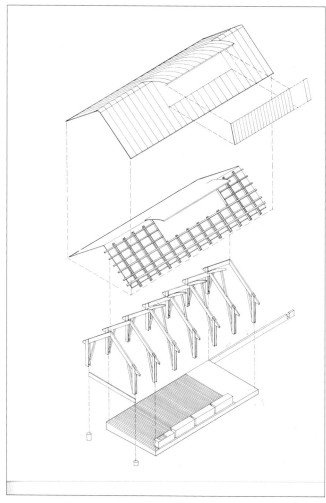

SECTIONS

SITE PLAN

PREVIOUS PAGES AND ABOVE:
Polycarbonate glazing on the
monitor and east-facing wall bring
in soft, diffused light during the day
and emit a warm glow at night.

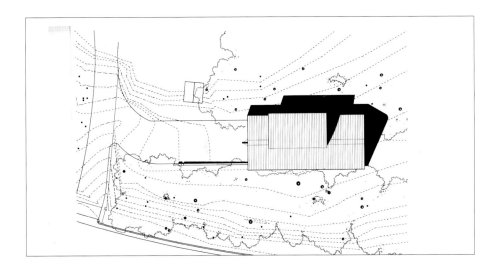

LEFT AND RIGHT: The interior is a skeleton of built-up wood frames within a metal skin.

LEFT: Roof detail RIGHT: Detail
of the polycarbonate glazing
on the east wall

RIGHT: The porch visually extends the interior space to the outside.

HONEY HOUSE

THE HONEY HOUSE SERVES A DUAL PURPOSE, AS AN 8-BY-24-FOOT structure for beekeeper processing and storing honey from the beehives, and as a single vehicle carport and sometimes outdoor work area. Inside are steel storage units, a work counter with processing equipment, and shelving. A steel plate and angled glass wall, oriented to the southeast, is used for displaying jars of honey. The glass wall also brings filtered light into the workspace through the jars, causing the honey to glow a deep amber. The building was fabricated in Arkansas, where the architect resides, and then shipped to the site in North Carolina where it was erected in three weeks. It is constructed of tongue-and-groove pine boards with a tubular steel frame.

ARCHITECT ▪ **MARLON BLACKWELL**
PHOTOGRAPHER ▪ **RICHARD LEO JOHNSON**
LOCATION ▪ **CASHIERS, NORTH CAROLINA**

SITE PLAN

AXONOMETRIC

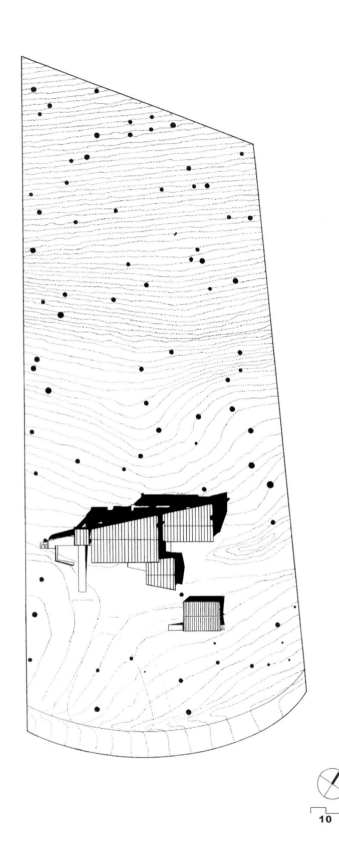

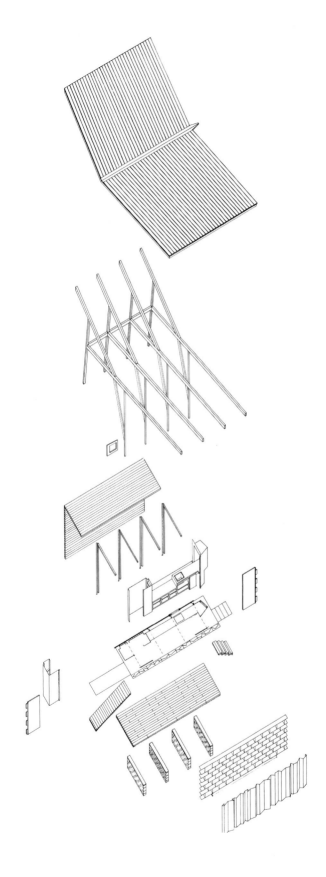

N

10 20

FLOOR PLAN

1. CARPORT
2. TOOL STORAGE
3. WORK AREA

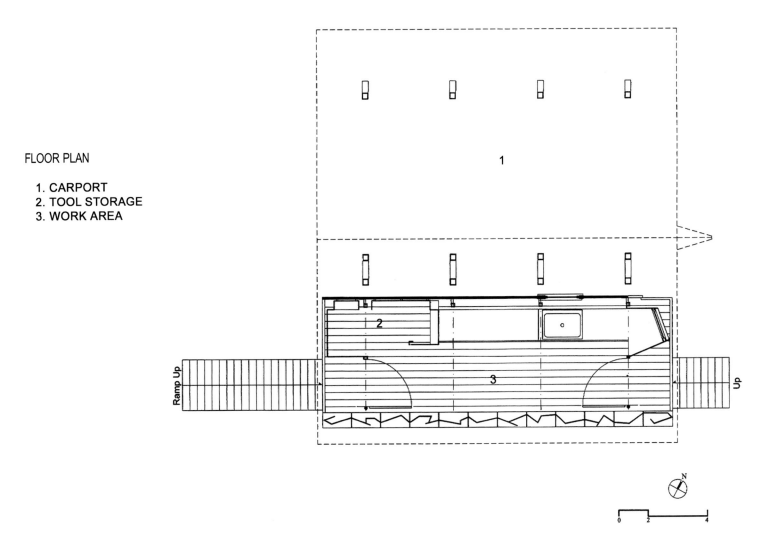

LEFT AND ABOVE: The honey wall is constructed of plate steel and glass.

LEFT: The glass wall serves a dual function as a display wall and as a source of natural light for the work area. BELOW: A detail of the steel and glass display wall

LEFT AND ABOVE: The roof flips up to create a carport,
which also functions as a work area for the beekeeper.

LEFT: The thin plate steel shelving is almost invisible when the wall is viewed straight on.

POOLSIDE DINING

THIS HOUSE OCCUPIES A THREE-ACRE SITE ON THE CONNECTICUT SHORE with a southern view of Long Island Sound. The program called for a year-round 7500-square-foot house, including decks and terraces that act as outdoor rooms and open-air corridors. A latticed deck surrounds the house and forms a base upon which sits a village of pavilions, each oriented toward their unique view: the living room enjoys an unobstructed view of the sea; the dining room looks southwest toward the Thimble Islands and summer sunsets; the study looks partly to sea and partly to the end of a rocky island; and the master bedroom looks to the quiet lee side of the nearby island. ■ The pool terrace is to the south where it looks out over Long Island Sound with uninterrupted views from principal spaces within the house. It is surrounded by a high latticed wall that provides definition for this outdoor room.

ARCHITECT ■ PAUL CHAID WITH SUSAN E. WYETH,
CENTERBROOK ARCHITECTS & PLANNERS
PHOTOGRAPHERS ■ ROBERT BENSON, MICK HALE
LOCATION ■ CONNECTICUT

SITE PLAN

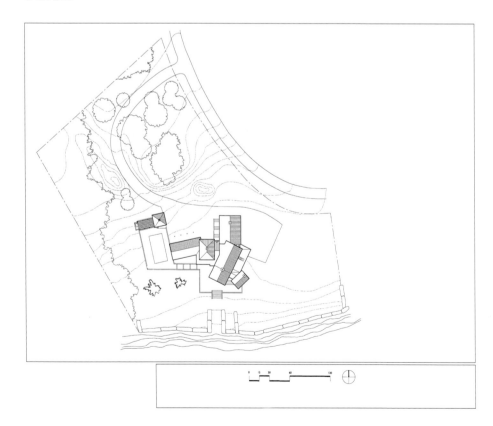

PREVIOUS PAGES: The outdoor dining room looks across the pool toward Long Island Sound. ABOVE: A view of the house from the sound RIGHT: The pool house is integrated into the lattice wall that defines the space around the pool.

WINE CELLAR

A PLACE TO BOTH ENJOY AND STORE WINE, THIS CELLAR IS TUCKED BENEATH a guest bedroom addition. The wine racks, tables, and pyramidal ceiling are constructed of jatoba wood, chosen for its aesthetic properties as well as its ability to withstand constant humidity. ■ With a total capacity of over 3,000 bottles, the wine cellar can accommodate an evolving collection. There are shelves for case storage, bins and racks for individual bottle storage, and display areas to showcase important wines. A concealed refrigerator under a side table stores champagne and white wines. An adjacent mechanical room, hidden behind a pivoting niche, keeps the entire cellar and case storage room at a constant temperature and humidity level. Neon and fiber optic lighting minimize heat and ultraviolet rays.

ARCHITECT ■ **MIRÓ RIVERA ARCHITECTS**
PHOTOGRAPHER ■ **CHRISTOPHER LOVI**
LOCATION ■ **AUSTIN, TEXAS**

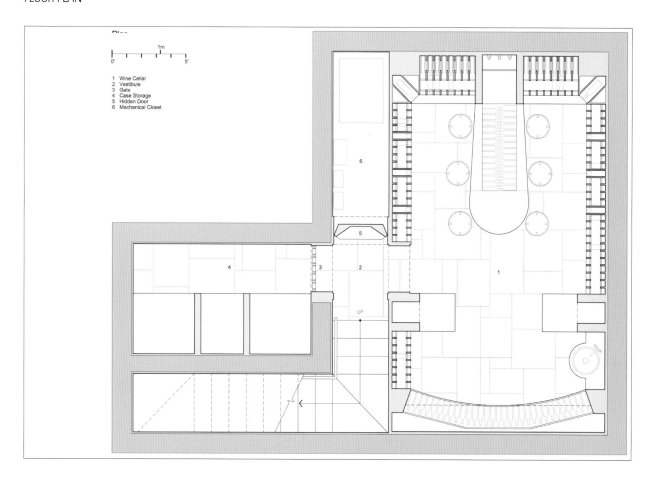

Plan

1m

0'   5'

1   Wine Cellar
2   Vestibule
3   Gate
4   Case Storage
5   Hidden Door
6   Mechanical Closet

PREVIOUS PAGES: The display table and jatoba stools provide an intimate setting for small dinner parties where guests can enjoy wine, food, company, and architecture. LEFT: A detail of the wine display shelving

SECTION

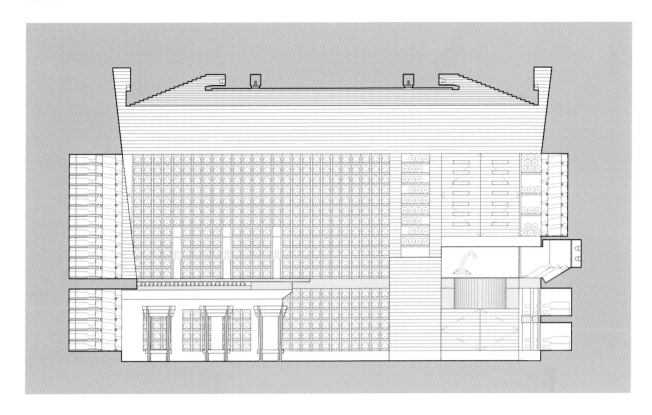

SECTION

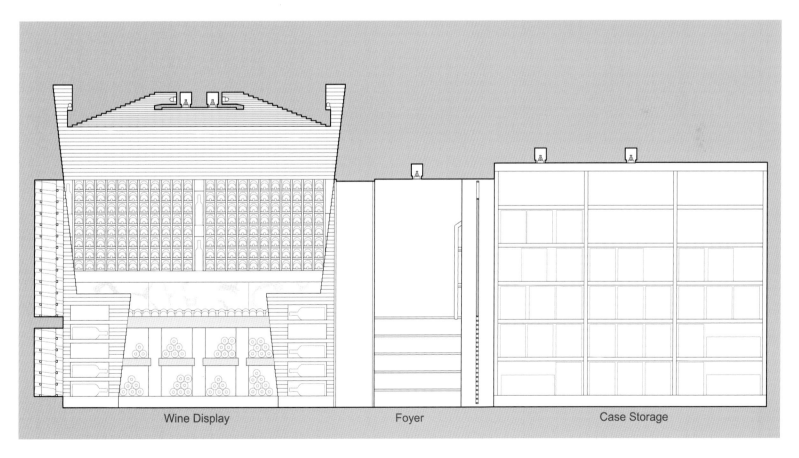

Wine Display   Foyer   Case Storage

LEFT AND BELOW RIGHT: Cocobola wood was used for the sink and table top, which is shown in its opened and closed positions. RIGHT: The carefully camouflaged refrigerator is used for storing champagne and white wines. FOLLOWING PAGES: The stairway leading to the cellar gives not clue as to what lies beyond.

ARCHITECT ▪ CENTERBROOK ARCHITECTS AND PLANNERS
ADDRESS ▪ 67 MAIN STREET
POST OFFICE BOX 655
CENTERBROOK, CT 06490
WWW.CENTERBROOK.COM

ARCHITECT ▪ EL DORADO, INC.
ADDRESS ▪ 1907C WYANDOTTE TRAFFICWAY
KANSAS CITY, MO 64108
WWW.ELDORADOARCHITECTS.COM

ARCHITECT ▪ FRANK HARMON ARCHITECT
ADDRESS ▪ 706 MOUNTFORD AVENUE
RALEIGH, NC 27603
WWW.FRANKHARMON.COM

ARCHITECT ▪ HANRAHAN MEYERS ARCHITECTS
ADDRESS ▪ 135 WEST 20TH STREET, SUITE 300
NEW YORK, NY 10011
WWW.HANRAHANMEYERS.COM

ARCHITECT ▪ LUNDBERG DESIGN
ADDRESS ▪ 2620 THIRD STREET
SAN FRANCISCO, CA 94107
WWW.LUNDBERGDESIGN.COM

ARCHITECT ▪ LAKE/FLATO ARCHITECTS
ADDRESS ▪ 311 THIRD STREET, SUITE 200
SAN ANTONIO, TX 78205
WWW.LAKEFLATO.COM

ARCHITECT ▪ MARLON BLACKWELL ARCHITECT
ADDRESS ▪ 100 WEST CENTER STREET, SUITE 001
FAYETTEVILLE, AK 72701
WWW.MARLONBLACKWELL.COM

ARCHITECT ▪ MIRÓ RIVERA ARCHITECTS
ADDRESS ▪ 505 POWELL STREET
SEATTLE, WA 98119
WWW.MIRORIVERA.COM

ARCHITECT ▪ PRENTISS ARCHITECTS
ADDRESS ▪ 224 WEST GALES
AUSTIN, TX 78703
WWW.PRENTISSARCH.COM

ARCHITECT ▪ SALMELA ARCHITECT
ADDRESS ▪ 852 GRANDVIEW AVENUE
DULUTH, MN 55812
WWW.SALMELAARCHITECT.COM

ARCHITECT ▪ SAMUEL H. WILLIAMSON ASSOCIATES

ADDRESS ▪ 120 NW NINTH AVENUE, SUITE 213

PORTLAND, OR 97209

WWW.SHWA.NET

ARCHITECT ▪ SHIPLEY ARCHITECTS

ADDRESS ▪ 5538 DYER STREET #107

DALLAS, TX 75206

WWW.SHIPLEYARCHITECTS.COM